Just Add Rum!

A Caribbean Cookbook

Starters & Light Fare
Tropical Drinks

by
Angela Spenceley

V.I. Cards, Inc.

Nisky Mailboxes P58 St. Thomas, USVI, 00802

Ph: (302) 774-2009

Writer@islands.vi

Design by Beatriz G. Mojarro

*This book is dedicated
to Roxanne for her unsurpassed
help in the kitchen.*

*Also, special thanks to
Gary Nelthopp of V.I. Rum Industries
for carefully explaining the rum distillation process to me.*

Contents

INTRODUCTION

J ust say rum and immediately Caribbean and Robert Louis Stevenson come to mind. Drunken pirates singing "Fifteen men on a dead man's chest and a bottle of rum" while burying chests of treasure on deserted islands. Picture oak rum barrels piled high in brick and molasses warehouses, traded alongside spices, cotton, indigo and other luxuries imported from all over the world by prosperous merchants. Transparent, turquoise-hued waters gently lap endless powder-white beaches. Palm trees, fanned by gentle tradewinds, cool the islands. Magenta bougainvillaea and hibiscus in scores of colors adorn pastel colored villas.

The West Indies make up more than 1,000 islands located in the Caribbean Sea. Some of the islands are bordered by the Atlantic on one side with the Caribbean on the other. Starting in the Florida Keys and ending at Venezuela, South America, they comprise three groups: Bahamas and the Greater and Lesser Antilles. The Windward and Leeward Islands, part of the Lesser Antilles, are volcanic, hence quite mountainous. Interesting that the name West Indies came from Christopher Columbus who discovered the islands in the late 15th century. Apparently Columbus and other Spanish explorers thought the islands were part of Asia, hence West Indies.

Columbus' most important contribution to the West Indies was the introduction of the sugar cane. Sugar cane was believed to have originated in New Guinea, traveled to China, India, and North Africa and made its way to Spain via the Canary Islands. Rum is an alcoholic drink, which can be produced from raw sugar cane juice or more commonly from sugarcane by-products, such as molasses. Molasses results when boiling crystallizes sugarcane juice.

Fermentation: The first alcoholic drinks were probably produced by accident, when someone left out some fresh juice and forgot about it. Fermentation is the process by which complex molecules, namely sugar, are broken down by yeast, enzymes or bacteria. The yeast uses up the sugar in the organic substance, produces alcohol and carbon dioxide. To distill means to trickle and purify. Think of spaghetti sauce cooking in a pot. When you lift the lid, water has accumulated and falls in drops, yet the water remains clear with very little to suggest that it came from spaghetti sauce. While distilling, liquids are heated until the element with the lowest boiling point has vaporized. This first distillation is water since it has the lowest boiling point. A second distillation occurs when the liquid remains over heat and the essential with the next boiling point has vaporized, hence a product with a much higher alcohol content.

Aging: Each island seems to have a different method and list of ingredients to produce rum, consequently the color, aroma, and flavor varies greatly. After fermentation and distillation, the rum is aged in oak casks. The aging came about quite by accident when ships traveling to Europe with West India rum absorbed some of the essence of the porous oak. The rums of Puerto Rico and the Virgin Islands are aged from one to four years producing a light, dry rum. Down-island, in Guadeloupe, rum is made from sugar cane juice, while in the Virgin Islands it is from molasses. *Jamaica's dark, heavy rum resembles sour-mash whiskey, produced from molasses and the addition of caramel during fermentation. This fermentation is quite long in retrospect, five to seven years.*

Rum production grew proportionately with the increase of sugar plantations in the West Indies. At one time, there were 114 working sugar mills on St. Croix, which rivaled only Barbados in sugar production. There is much speculation about the origin of the word "rum", but it may have come from the English word, rumbullion, meaning a great disturbance or melee as we like to say in the Caribbean. The Molasses Act, enacted by the British in 1733, imposed a heavy tariff on molasses, rum, and sugar imported from sources other than British West Indies. Americans financially preferred to conduct business with the French West Indies and this controversy led to the American Revolution.

Blending: *Much rum today is blended to produce quite superior results. Blending can be accomplished by using different rums, different casks, aging for different periods of time or even adding herbs, fruits and spices.*

Some rums are ideal for drinks with fruit juices, others taste much better on the rocks, with a splash of water and twist of lime. The only way to find out truly is to experiment. Try each food and drink recipe several times, varying the brand of rum. Make notes in this cookbook about the most popular results and above all enjoy the rich satisfying flavor of true Caribbean rum!

SOUPS

SOUPS

an Introduction

Just mention the word soup and all sorts of memories are evoked. Soup was a treat when we were kids. It was aromatic, filled the tummy and usually did not have any hated vegetables added to it. If it did, they were easy to pick out.

Soup is the answer to today's busy, harried families that require meals that are facile in preparation and nutritious. All four of the food groups can easily be incorporated into soup. Soup is also easy to stretch when the occasional surprise guest turns up. Serve with a complimentary salad and an mélange of breads and crackers.

Long live the era of the soup!

SOUPS

SPICY TOMATO SOUP
Dominican Republic

YIELD: 6 SERVINGS

The Dominican Republic occupies two-thirds of the island of Hispaniola and its capital, Santo Domingo, is the oldest continuously inhabited city in the Western Hemisphere. History buffs as well as beach lovers seek out the island. La Romana is the longest stretch of beach in the Caribbean and Pixo Duarte (10,128 feet) is the highest peak in the West Indies. Dining on the island is a rather formal affair, taken quite seriously. There are several local rums, Barcelo, Bermudez, and Brugal, which are used liberally in the local cuisine.

3 pounds fresh ripe tomatoes, seeded and chopped	¼ cup chopped cilantro juice of one lemon
1 tablespoon sun-dried tomato paste	½ teaspoon lemon zest ½ teaspoon ground cumin
1 small white onion, minced	½ teaspoon ground coriander
1 small mildly fiery chili pepper, seeded and minced	4 cups chicken stock ¼ cup light golden rum
½ stalk celery, minced	2 tablespoons extra-virgin olive
2 cloves garlic, crushed	oil

. . . .

In a medium saucepan, preferably steel, sauté the onion, peppers, celery and garlic until the onion turns clear. Do not brown.

Stir in all other ingredients except the rum. Bring to a gentle boil for 8 to 10 minutes. Reduce the heat, add the rum, cook for another 10 minutes. Slow, low heat is the key here. Remove from heat and allow cooling.

Pour the soup into a blender, purée coarsely so it remains chunky. Return to sauce pan and gently reheat. Serve with crunchy Portuguese or French bread.

GRILLED RED PEPPER SOUP
with RUM CREAM
The Grenadines

YIELD: 6 SERVINGS

The Grenadines are quiet little islands located far down in the chain of islands known as the Windward Islands. This is the place for quiet, elegant evening dining. The peppers may be either roasted on the barbecue grill or indoors in a 400° oven for 35 to 40 minutes. Also note that extra heads of garlic may also be roasted and used to spread on buttered and toasted rounds of French bread.

2	entire heads of garlic		*rum cream:*
6	large red bell peppers, seeded and cut in wide strips	½	cup crème fraiche or sour cream
3	large ripe tomatoes	¼	freshly grated Romano cheese
½	cup minced red onion	3	tablespoons chopped parsley
	olive oil	2	tablespoons dark rum
6	cups chicken stock		salt and ground pepper to taste

. . . .

Pre-heat the barbecue grill. Brush the garlic, pepper strips and tomatoes with olive oil. Wrap the garlic in foil and place along with other vegetables on the grill. Grill vegetables over high heat for 3 minutes per side. Leave garlic on until soft, another 20 minutes.

While the garlic roasts, heat 1 tablespoon of the olive oil in a large saucepan. Sauté the onion until clear. Add the stock and roasted vegetables, bringing to a simmer. Remove garlic from the grill and squeeze out the garlic paste from the cloves. Simmer over low heat for 10 minutes. Remove from heat and allow to sit for 30 minutes. Pour into a blender and purée until smooth. Return to saucepan and reheat.

To make rum cream, whisk together all ingredients in a small bowl. Ladle the soup into bowl, adding a dollop of rum cream to the top. Serve with buttered toasted French bread.

CURRIED CHICKEN SOUP
with PHYLLO CRUST

Turks and Caicos

YIELD: 6 SERVINGS

This British Crown Colony is a haven for banking and insurance institutions as well as for divers who explore the off-shore reef formations of its 40 islands. Dining is a relaxed play on local Caribbean produce and the best of imported stateside treats.

2 tablespoons light vegetable oil	1 stalk celery, minced
3 cloves garlic, crushed	1 cup frozen peas
½ cup shallots, chopped	6 cups chicken stock
1 small vidalia onion, minced	¼ cup light rum
1 tablespoon freshly grated ginger	1½ cups cooked & cubed chicken meat
1 tablespoon curry powder	8-10 sheets phyllo dough
½ teaspoon cinnamon	melted butter
¼ teaspoon nutmeg	salt and pepper
1 large carrot, peeled & thinly sliced	

· · · · · · · · · ·

In a small pan heat the curry and spices until slightly toasted and aroma is given off. Use a dry pan and wooden spoon to stir. This releases the true flavor of the curry. In a large deep saucepan, sauté the shallots, onion, ginger, garlic and celery until the onion is clear.

Add the chicken stock, carrot, celery and spices bringing to a boil. Reduce to a simmer, adding the chicken meat. Cook until carrots are tender, stirring in the rum last.

Preheat oven to 375° and pour soup into ovenproof bowls. Layer the phyllo, brushing with butter between the layers. Sprinkle very lightly with salt and pepper. Tuck the phyllo around the bowl edges, brushing the top of the dough also with butter. Cut several slits as one would a pie. Bake until tops are golden. Serve at once.

GINGERED CARROT
and
MANGO SOUP
St. Lucia

YIELD: 4 SERVINGS

One of our housekeepers was from St. Lucia. It seemed she was always homesick for her beautiful island. Visitors to the island are delighted by a rainforest that covers a good deal of the island, sulfur springs from a long-dormant volcano and the sight of the island's twin peaks, the Pitons which rise from the sea to above 2,400 feet. Serve this soup as a first course during al fresco dinner parties.

4	*large carrots, peeled, sliced and steamed until tender*
1	*cup fresh ripe mango, cubed*
1	*tablespoon freshly grated ginger*
¼	*cup Mango-Passion Chutney*
½	*teaspoon curry powder*
2	*cups chicken stock*
2	*tablespoons golden rum*
	juice of one lemon

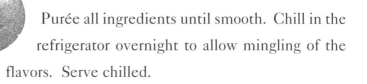

Purée all ingredients until smooth. Chill in the refrigerator overnight to allow mingling of the flavors. Serve chilled.

PUMPKIN LIME SOUP
Dominica

YIELD: 6 SERVINGS

Dominica was another one of those islands that we visited while on a cruise ship. I may have mentioned this before, but while the ship itself was gorgeous, the food was most unappealing. Needless to say, the first order of the day while ashore was to find an exemplary meal. The hostess of this restaurant was kind enough to part with this recipe. Oh, by the way, Dominica is a volcanic island with dark, not white sand beaches. Lovely.

4	cups fresh chicken stock	½	teaspoon thyme
1	stalk of celery	½	teaspoon ground cinnamon
1	large carrot, peeled and thinly sliced		juice of one lime
1	large onion, minced	1	teaspoon lime zest
4	cloves garlic, crushed	2	tablespoons lime rum
2	pounds pumpkin or butternut squash, peeled, seeded and cubed	1	cup heavy cream

· · · · · · · · · ·

In a deep stockpot, combine the chicken stock, celery, carrot, onion, garlic, pumpkin, thyme, and cinnamon. Bring to a boil, reduce heat to a simmer. Cook until vegetables are just tender. Do not overcook.

Remove the celery and carrot, discarding. Pour small amounts of the stock and pumpkin into a blender, purée until smooth.

Return to pot, adding the lime, lime zest, and rum. Reheat gently. Slowly stir in the cream, but do not boil. Serve at once with baguettes or garlic toast points.

BAHAMIAN SEAFOOD CHOWDER

Nassau

YIELD: 10 TO 12 SERVINGS

*H*aving originally come from New England and having summered on Nantucket, I have a profound fondness for clam chowder. After living in the Caribbean for over 15 years, I have managed to add fiery chili peppers to nearly every dish. This chowder is no exception. Have plenty of ice-cold beer on hand. Enjoy!

2	pounds chopped clams, fresh, rozen or canned	2	large ripe tomatoes, chopped
1	pound lobster meat	4	tablespoons chopped cilantro
1	pound scallops	¼	teaspoon cinnamon
1	pound shrimp	1	bay leaf
3	quarts water	¼	teaspoon nutmeg
1	quart vegetable broth	¼	teaspoon allspice
3	stalks celery, coarsely chopped	¼	teaspoon mace
2	large carrots, peeled and sliced	1	teaspoon sea salt
6	cloves garlic, crushed	2	tablespoons cracked black pepper
3	jalapeño peppers, seeded and minced		juice of one lemon
4	tablespoons vegetable oil	¼	cup dark rum
1	large onion, minced	3	cups light cream
3	large potatoes, peeled & cubed	½	cup flour
		½	cup peanut oil

continued

Reserve the liquid from the clams if using canned and add to the 4 quarts of water. Make the roux and set aside as follows: Heat the oil in a large heavy skillet. After the oil is hot, remove the skillet from the heat. Whisk in the flour until no lumps remain. Return to very low heat, stir constantly until a light brown color and nutty aroma is given off. Remove from heat at once, allow cooling. Roux may be kept in the refrigerator for several weeks or frozen. It imparts a wonderful nutty flavor to soups and is used as a thickener for sauces also.

In a large stockpot, heat the oil and sauté the onions, garlic, celery, peppers and spices until the onions turn clear. Add water and clams to this mixture and bring to a boil. Reduce the heat, remove ½ cup broth from pot. Whisk in the roux until smooth.

Add the potatoes and cook for 8 to 10 minutes. Add all other remaining ingredients, except the rum. Cook for an additional 10 minutes. Finally add in the rum, cook 5 more minutes. Remove from heat for 10 minutes. Stir in the cream, but do not cook. Serve at once.

151 BLACK BEAN SOUP

Puerto Rico

YIELD: 4 TO 6 SERVINGS

Yes, you guessed it! We are using 151 proof rum in this recipe. Puerto Rico has many excellent, well known rums such as Barcadi, Don Q and Ron Rico.

Black beans are to Puerto Rico what hot dogs are to ball games. Try this soup as a filling first course.

2	cups cooked black beans with liquid reserved
4	cloves garlic, crushed
½	small habanero pepper, seeded and minced
½	cup white minced onion
¼	teaspoon allspice
¼	teaspoon cinnamon
¼	cup 151 proof rum
¼	cup fresh pineapple, finely minced
1	tablespoon olive oil
	salt and pepper to taste

. . . .

In a small stockpot heat the oil and sauté the garlic and habanero pepper for 5 minutes. Deglaze the pan by swishing around the 151 proof rum. Add the spices and pineapple, simmering for 2 more minutes.

Add the beans and their liquid. Continue cooking over low heat for 15 to 20 minutes. Remove from heat and serve with a dollop of sour cream.

This soup also reheats nicely as the flavors have had a chance to settle.

AVOCADO PINEAPPLE SOUP

St. Thomas

YIELD: 4 SERVINGS

Ah, St. Thomas, gorgeous island of mountains, glistening beaches and oh, the shopping! A chef who has since left the island reluctantly gave the following to me, but memories of wonderful meals remain.

3	*large avocados, peeled, seeded and cubed*
½	*cup fresh pineapple chunks*
	juice of one lemon and one lime
1	*tablespoon pineapple rum*
½	*cup sweet potato, cubed and boiled*
	sprinkle of nutmeg and cinnamon
1	*cup low-fat vanilla yogurt*

. . . .

Purée all ingredients slowly in the blender. If done too quickly, unattractive air bubbles arise giving the soup the appearance of a smoothie.

Pour into the prettiest soup bowls that you can find and garnish each with a fresh pineapple slice. With a light hand sprinkle with nutmeg and cinnamon.

LENTIL AND CHICKEN DUMPLING SOUP

St. Maarten

YIELD: 8 TO 10 SERVINGS

My 11 year old daughter absolutely loves dumplings in her chicken soup. Whenever we go out to one of those little out-of-the way West Indian restaurants, the request is for chicken soup. Oh, and by the way, does it have dumplings in it? The arrival of dumplings in the Caribbean is a direct result of European influence. This recipe comes from the Dutch side of St. Maarten. St. Maarteen/St. Martin is very similar to St. Thomas in some ways. Geographically it does not have the rolling green hills, but there is an abundance of duty-free shopping and restaurants too numerous to mention.

soup:

2	tablespoons safflower or other light vegetable oil
1	medium yellow onion, minced
2	cloves garlic crushed
1	carrot, peeled and very thinly sliced, no big fat rounds here
¼	teaspoon ground cinnamon
¼	teaspoon allspice
¼	teaspoon nutmeg
2	cups lentils (red ones look pretty)
6	cups chicken stock
½	cup vegetable stock
½	cup golden rum
	salt and freshly ground pepper to taste

continued

dumplings:

2	tablespoons clarified butter (clarified butter will not burn while sautéing)
¼	cup minced yellow onion
1	garlic clove crushed
¼	teaspoon nutmeg
1	teaspoon Tabasco® pepper sauce
½	teaspoon sea salt
½	teaspoon freshly ground black pepper
½	pound chicken breast, deboned and chopped
½	cup breadcrumbs
2	eggs
1	tablespoon sour cream

. . . .

To make the dumplings, run all the dumpling ingredients through a food processor until smooth. Chill in the refrigerator until firm. Form into tiny balls about 1 inch or so in diameter. Drop into boiling water. Lower the heat and continue to simmer. When cooked, dumplings will rise to the surface. Carefully use tongs to remove them, shake to drain the water, and reserve on a ceramic plate.

In a deep soup or stockpot, sauté the onions and garlic in the oil until clear. Add in the dry spices and cook for another minute. Add all other remaining ingredients and cook until the lentils are soft. Some lentils take less time than others to cook, so test for doneness frequently or you will have lentil mush. Add the dumplings and serve at once with a dollop of sour cream and freshly ground pepper.

ORANGE SWEET POTATO
and
LOBSTER BISQUE
Cayman Islands

YIELD: 6 TO 8 SERVINGS

The Cayman Islands are located in the Eastern Caribbean, past Cuba, heading towards Jamaica. Grand Cayman has the most fascinating turtle farm (turtle meat is eaten here). There are turtles of all sizes, or rather ages. The babies look like the pet turtles we had as children, yet they grow into these enormous adults with heads the size of a grown human being. Oh, and the noise they make when they come up to gulp air is deafening. Serve this delicately hued soup during the chilly winter months. Interestingly, it can also be served in the summer, chilled.

5	pounds sweet potatoes or yams, peeled and cubed	5	cups chicken stock
2	tablespoons clarified butter	1	cup vegetable stock
1	small onion, minced	¼	up roux (see Bahamian Seafood Chowder)
2	cloves garlic, crushed	¼	cup dark rum
¼	serrano pepper, seeded and minced	1	teaspoon orange zest
1	teaspoon fresh tarragon, chopped	11 ½	pounds lobster
¼	teaspoon cinnamon	1	cup heavy cream or ½ sour cream and ½ heavy cream
¼	teaspoon nutmeg		sour cream
			capers

continued

. . . .

In a deep soup pot, sauté the onion, garlic and serrano pepper in the butter until the onion is just clear. Add the tarragon and the spices and gently cook another minute or so.

Add the chicken and vegetable stocks with the yams, and bring to a boil. Reduce the heat and cook for 20 minutes. Remove one cup of the liquid and stir in the roux until no lumps remain. Return to the stockpot and stir in thoroughly. Add the lobster and cook over medium heat for another 10 minutes. Remove from heat and allow to cool for 20 minutes. Take the lobster out of the pot, and proceed to remove the meat. Chop into chunks.

Purée the stock one blenderful at a time until smooth. Return to low heat in the stockpot. Stir in the rum, orange zest and heavy cream. Do not boil, as something unattractive will happen to the cream. When reheated, serve at once in pretty soup bowls. Garnish with a dollop of sour cream and capers.

LEMON-RUM CREAM OF TOMATO SOUP

Aruba

YIELD: 4 TO 6 SERVINGS

I liked Aruba when we stopped there on our cruise. The little city was immaculate, charmingly colorful and the epitome of the Caribbean. Nearly all the hotels, shops and restaurants sit on one strip. The dining was beyond wonderful. This is another good recipe to use that citrus rum with.

1	tablespoon peanut oil	3	pounds firm, ripe tomatoes, chopped and seeded
1	small onion minced		
3	cloves garlic, crushed	1	tablespoon sun-dried tomato paste
2	cups chicken stock		
2	cups vegetable stock	2	tablespoons fresh basil, chopped
	juice of two lemons		
1	teaspoon lemon zest	1	cup light cream or half and half
2	tablespoons citrus rum		
			salt and pepper to taste

. . . .

In a deep soup pot, heat the oil and sauté the onion and garlic. Pour in the stocks and bring to a boil. Reduce heat and stir in lemon juice, zest, rum, and tomatoes. Bring to a simmer and remove one cup of the broth. Stir in the sun-dried tomato paste and fresh basil. Cook slowly for another 15 minutes.

Remove from heat and fold in the cream. Serve immediately with oyster crackers or another water cracker.

CHILLED PASSIONFRUIT
and
DILLED SHRIMP SOUP
British Virgin Islands

YIELD: 4 TO 6 SERVINGS

Tortola resembles St. Thomas 25 years ago, with its enchanting gingerbread West Indian cottages, donkeys on the side of the road and generally laid-back tranquil atmosphere. Virgin Gorda is probably like what Tortola was 25 years ago. The British Virgin Islands consist of approximately 50 cays, islets and islands with gently rolling green hills and spectacular vistas of the chain of islands. This recipe is quite exploratory as it combines Passionfruit liqueur with just a hint of coconut rum.

3	Passionfruit *(I see more of these sometimes in state side groceries than I do in the Caribbean due to shipping availability)*	2	medium ripe papayas, seeded and chopped
3	tablespoons Passionfruit liqueur	2	cups chicken stock
		1	pound cooked shrimp, chopped
1	tablespoon coconut rum	12	cooked, shelled jumbo shrimp
2	tablespoons light rum	1	tablespoon fresh dill, chopped
			salt and freshly ground pepper to taste

. . . .

Cut the Passionfruit in two and hollow out the seeds and pulp. Purée the pulp and seeds in 1 cup of the chicken broth.

Add all other ingredients to the food processor or the blender except the shrimp, reserving this until last. Add several tablespoons of the shrimp and purée. Fold in the remaining shrimp chunks, but do not purée.

Serve in individual bowls and garnish sides of bowl with shrimp.

HOTTER THAN HELL
BEEF CHILI SOUP

St. Thomas

YIELD: 4 SERVINGS

In A Taste of the Virgin Islands, I went into detail regarding the culinary history of the Virgin Islands. From the Danish, British, East Indian and African influence to the occasional Hispanic, I never did mention the modern day influence of our local chapter of the Texas Society. Every year there is a chili cookoff where professional and amateur cooks alike test their skills of fire. The following recipe with its hearty rum kick is sure to be a crowd pleaser.

1	pound extra-lean ground beef	1	16-ounce can tomatoes, drained and chopped
1	large yellow onion, minced		
3	cloves garlic, crushed	4	tablespoons sun-dried tomato paste
1	large green bell pepper, seeded and chopped		
		½	small can regular tomato paste
1	large red bell pepper, seeded and chopped		
		2	tablespoons apple-cider vinegar
1	habañero pepper, seeded and minced		
		¼	cup dark rum
1	jalapeno pepper, seeded and minced	1	16-ounce can black beans
		3	teaspoons chili powder
1	tablespoon olive oil	1	teaspoon fresh basil
½	cup hot water, more as needed	1	cup chopped fresh ripe tomatoes
			salt and pepper to taste

continued

· · · · · · · · · ·

In a large frying pan with a lid, fry the hamburger meat until thoroughly cooked and no pink remains. Use the lid to avoid splattering the entire kitchen. Drain in a colander and rinse with very hot water. This removes a good portion of the fat and calories, yet leaves the flavor. Return this to a pot large enough to hold the chili.

In a small separate pan, sauté onion, garlic and all the peppers in the olive oil until the onion is clear. Turn this into the meat and stir in the tomatoes, tomato pastes, vinegar, beans, chili powder, basil and hot water. Add more hot water as needed as the mixture cooks down and adjust according to how thick the chili is desired. Bring to a boil and reduce heat to a simmer. Cook for 20 minutes.

Serve hot with a large spoonful of chopped fresh tomatoes.

ROSEMARY LAMB STEW

Barbados

YIELD: 4 SERVINGS

At the end of May, the Barbados Caribbean Jazz Festival is held in Bridgetown for three days. While attending this lively feast, I came across this fragrant stew. Make a couple of days ahead for peak flavor.

1	pound lamb stew meat
1	tablespoon light vegetable oil
3	garlic cloves, crushed
2	large potatoes, peeled and cubed
2	large carrots, peeled and cubed
1	stalk celery, chopped
1	small onion, minced
1	cup beef stock
1	cup vegetable stock
½	cup dark rum
½	cup roux (see Bahamian Seafood Chowder)
2	tablespoons fresh rosemary, chopped
1	bay leaf
½	teaspoon marjoram
¼	teaspoon cinnamon

. . . .

In a large saucepan, brown the lamb in the vegetable oil. Drain the fat and press with white paper towels. Add the stocks, rum, spices and vegetables. Cover, bring to a boil and reduce heat. Cook for about 20 minutes until vegetables are tender.

Remove one cup of the broth and whisk in the roux until smooth. Return to pot, stirring well. Serve at once.

PORK AND NAVY BEAN SOUP

Puerto Rico

YIELD: 4 SERVINGS

Pork came to Puerto Rico via Columbus and the Spaniards and is still extremely popular on *La Isla de Encanto* today. Puerto Rico is an amazing amalgamation of rich cultural history and arts, ancient fortresses heavy with Spanish influence, rainforest, rivers, mountains and palm-rimmed beaches. Let's not forget the Miami Beach look of Isla Verde and the Condado with its high rises and glittering casinos in San Juan. Olé!

1	pound cubed pork (a portion of this, about ¼ may be smoked for added flavor)	1	tablespoon coarse sea salt
		¼	cup chopped red bell pepper
1	cup navy beans, soaked overnight	¼	cup chopped fresh cilantro
		¼	cup chopped fresh oregano
2	cups vegetable broth	2	tablespoons 151 proof rum
2	cups water	1	tablespoon sun-dried tomato paste
4	tablespoons oil		fresh tomatoes
1	medium onion, minced		sour cream
3	garlic cloves		mortar and pestle
2	tablespoons freshly ground pepper		

. . . .

First, let's make the traditional Puerto Rican staple condiment called sofrito. Using the mortar and pestle, take 2 tablespoons of the olive oil and add in the salt and pepper in the center of the mortar. Use an up and down grinding motion, pulverize the two. Next, add in the garlic and grind to a paste. Do the same with each of the following ingredients, one at a time, until a fragrant paste has formed: bell pepper, cilantro, oregano and tomato paste. Set aside.

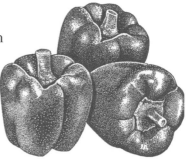

In the remaining two tablespoons of the oil, brown the pork. Drain off all excess fat.

In a large deep pot, bring the water and vegetable broth to a boil. Add beans and simmer for 30 minutes. Add the meat and sofrito cook for an additional 30 minutes, until beans are soft. Add rum and cook for 5 more minutes.

Serve hot with a crisp green salad on the side and plenty of hot bread.

RUM AND CHEESE SOUP

St. Martin

YIELD: 4 SERVINGS

St. Martin is famous for its Dutch Gouda cheese. Whenever my husband and I travel to St. Martin, we always pick up an enormous wheel of cheese at the airport on our way home. Lunch at the airport consists of grilled Gouda cheese sandwiches. Through experience, we learned to cut up the cheese, freeze a portion for later use and give the rest away before our waistlines expanded too much!

1½	cups shredded Gouda cheese
1	cup chicken stock
¼	cup vegetable stock
¼	cup light rum
1	tablespoon chopped pimentos
¼	cup minced celery
¼	cup minced red onion
1	garlic clove, minced
½	jalapeno pepper, minced
3	tablespoons roux (see Bahamian Seafood Chowder)
1½	cups milk
	salt and pepper to taste

. . . .

In a medium saucepan, bring to a simmer broths, rum, celery, garlic and onion. Cook until the onions and celery are soft. Remove one cup of the broth and stir in the roux. Return this to the pot.

Cook for several minutes until thickened. Gradually fold in grated cheese, gently cooking until cheese is melted. Stir in the chopped pimentos.

Serve with plenty of bread for dipping in this fondue-like soup.

APPETIZERS
&
LIGHT FARE

APPETIZERS

an Introduction

No matter what your needs are, be it a light first course, appetizers for an intimate affair for two or hor d'oevres for the company Christmas party, the following recipes will add style and flair to your affair.

Each island in the Caribbean seems to have some variation on the fritter. Feel free to substitute sweet potato , pumpkin , zucchini, conch, or seafood with these fritters. Have plenty of island-style hot sauce and chutney on hand to accompany these.

Be sure to serve hot appetizers, hot, and cold ones, cold. Choose appetizers that compliment each other such as Banana Rum Fritters and Curried Crab and Pear Dip. Select light Calypso or Reggae music to impart a Caribbean air. Of course, in the summer you will want to have your party outside with softly glowing candle footlights. In the cooler months, safely bring the gathering indoors and create a balmy equatorial atmosphere with potted palms, arrangements of bird-of-paradise and ginger and an assortment of freely flowing rums from the islands.

Welcome to de islands, mon!

APPETIZERS

BANANA RUM FRITTERS
Virgin Islands

YIELD: 4 to 6 appetizer servings

Fritters really make wonderful finger food. They can be spicy or they can be dessert-like. Some, like the Banana Rum Fritters can go either way – serve with a fiery hot sauce or a mild chutney.

1	*cup flour*
¼	*cup sugar*
½	*teaspoon salt*
½	*teaspoon baking powder*
½	*teaspoon nutmeg*
1	*teaspoon vanilla extract*
1	*egg*
3	*cups mashed, ripe bananas*
¼	*cup banana rum*
¾	*cup water*
¼	*teaspoon cinnamon*
	vegetable oil for frying

. . . .

In a heavy glass bowl, combine all the dry ingredients mixing well. Separately whisk together the remaining ingredients except for the oil. Blend the dry and the wet ingredients together and refrigerate for an hour.

Heat the oil to 375°. Drop the batter in by large spoonfuls and fry until golden. Drain on white paper towels to absorb the fat. Fritters may be rolled in granulated sugar or served with Junkanoo Hot Sauce (recipe follows).

JUNKANOO HOT SAUCE

Nassau

YIELD: 2 cups

The first time that I saw and heard Junkanoo was in Nassau, Bahamas. My husband and I were at a convention, which held a party on an islet in the harbor. The closing festivities involved what appeared to me as grounded Mocko Jumbis. These fantastic creatures with bells on their ankles, elaborate headdresses, glitz and feathers, violently blew whistles, clanked steel pans and shook noisemakers. The sound exploded all around us and it made our Calypso music sound sedate in comparison. Hence the title for this explosive hot sauce was quite appropriate!

6	*large habañero, seeded and minced*
1	*large yellow onion, chopped finely*
1	*red bell pepper, seeded and chopped*
½	*cup cauliflower florets*
5	*cloves of garlic*
½	*cup stewed canned tomatoes*
1	*tablespoon brown sugar*
1	*tablespoon safflower oil*
¼	*cup gold rum*
1	*bottle of white vinegar*
1	*sterilized jar or canning bottle to hold hot sauce*

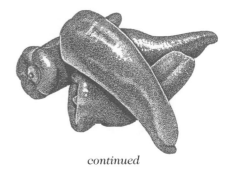

continued

. . . .

Lightly sauté the peppers, onion and garlic in the oil, set aside. Steam the carrots and the cauliflower until just tender.

Take 1 cup of the white vinegar and stir in the brown sugar. Fill the sterilized jar with the pepper mixture and steamed vegetables. Add the stewed tomatoes. Try to be artistic about this and create pretty layers. Pour the vinegar over the top of this, adding more vinegar if necessary.

Seal the jar tightly and plunge into a pot of boiling water to aid in the canning process. I always like to refrigerate my sauces and chutneys since we live in the heat of the Caribbean, however a cool basement will do as well.

Allow to sit for two weeks. Serve with fritters, fish, jerked meats, even pizza or spaghetti. The sauce may be puréed in the blender. Beware of the fire!

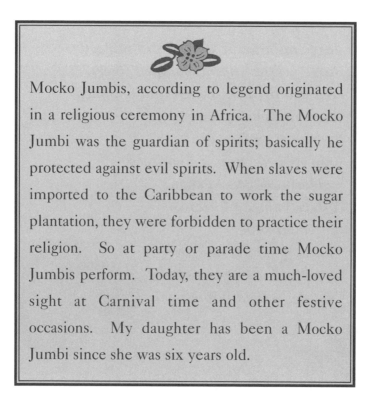

Mocko Jumbis, according to legend originated in a religious ceremony in Africa. The Mocko Jumbi was the guardian of spirits; basically he protected against evil spirits. When slaves were imported to the Caribbean to work the sugar plantation, they were forbidden to practice their religion. So at party or parade time Mocko Jumbis perform. Today, they are a much-loved sight at Carnival time and other festive occasions. My daughter has been a Mocko Jumbi since she was six years old.

PINEAPPLE and CRAB MUSHROOMS

Guadeloupe

YIELD: 6 to 8 appetizer servings

I was on a cruise a couple of years ago when we stopped in Guadeloupe. The ship was new and beautiful, but the food was terrible. We were traveling with several other couples and all of us were disappointed with shipboard dining. At any rate, we found the most wonderful place to lunch on this pretty little island and concluded a trip with the most congenial of friends. Voilà, the mushroom caps!

1	pound lump crabmeat, with cartilage picked out	2	tablespoons fresh parsley, chopped
1	small onion, minced	1	cup Italian-style breadcrumbs
2	cloves garlic, minced	2	tablespoons safflower oil
¼	cup green bell pepper, minced	1	tablespoon butter
¼	cup fresh or canned pineapple, finely chopped	1	tablespoon gold rum
			fresh ground pepper
¼	cup fresh mushrooms, finely chopped	36 - 48	mushroom caps, depending on size

· · · · · · · · · ·

Preheat oven to 350°.

Sauté the onions, garlic, pepper and mushrooms in the oil until the onions are just clear. Add the shredded crab, pineapple and parsley and sauté over low heat for one more minute.

Add the butter, breadcrumbs, rum and ground pepper to taste. Remove from heat and fill the mushroom caps, baking for 15 minutes.

Serve at once with a spoonful of Mango-Passion Chutney.

MANGO-PASSION CHUTNEY
British Virgin Islands

YIELD: 36 ounces

I travel to the British Virgin Islands at least once a month. There is this wonderful hole-in-the-wall restaurant complete with chickens freely roaming through it that serves roti. One day the owner took me aside and shared this chutney with me. I managed to coax the recipe from her and here it is.

4	large, under-ripe mangoes, peeled, seeded and cubed
1	tablespoon fresh grated ginger
¼	cup minced onions
2	cloves garlic, minced
½	teaspoon cinnamon
¼	teaspoon cloves
1 - 2	habañero peppers, seeded and minced to taste
½	cup golden raisins
2	cups granulated sugar
1	cup white vinegar
½	cup water
¼	cup white rum
¼	cup passionfruit liqueur
1	teaspoon sea salt
2	medium-sized canning jars

. . . .

In a large steel pot, bring the vinegar and water to a boil. Add the mango, ginger, onion, garlic, peppers, raisins, sugar and spices, returning to a boil. Remove from heat, allow to sit so that the fruit can soak up the vinegar and sugar.

Return to heat and simmer for 40 minutes. Do not overcook as the sugar will caramelize and overpower the flavor of the mango. Remove from heat and stir in the rum and passionfruit liqueur.

Pour into sterilized containers, sealing tightly. Plunge into boiling water to can. Keeps for up to 12 weeks in the refrigerator.

Serve with fritters, Pineapple and Crab Mushrooms, roti, fish, chicken or meat dishes.

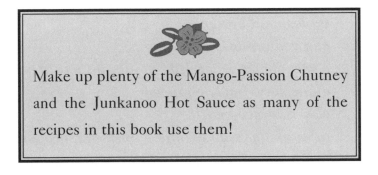

Make up plenty of the Mango-Passion Chutney and the Junkanoo Hot Sauce as many of the recipes in this book use them!

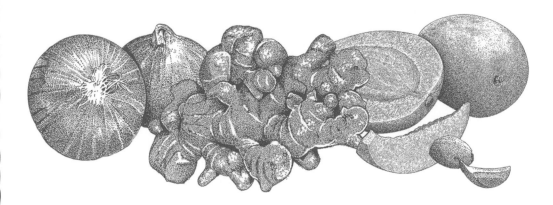

CURRIED CRAB and PEAR DIP

St. Martin, West Indies

YIELD: 6 to 8 appetizer servings

This is an example of a beautiful Caribbean marriage of flavors. The delicate sweetness of the pear, the aroma of the citrus rum and the fire of the spices combine to form an exotic taste sensation. Serve this when you truly wish to impress your guests.

1	pound lump crab meat with cartilage removed
1	tablespoon butter
¼	cup red onion, finely chopped
1	large ripe pear, peeled, cored and cut in small cubes
¼	cup celery, finely chopped
2	cloves minced garlic
3	tablespoons well chopped fresh mushrooms
½	teaspoon minced scotch bonnet pepper or any other fiery pepper
2	tablespoons capers
½	teaspoon fresh lemon zest
¼	cup plain breadcrumbs
¼	cup mayonnaise
4	tablespoons citrus rum
1	tablespoon Calvados
1	tablespoon curry powder, as fresh as possible
1	egg, lightly beaten
	fresh ground pepper and salt to taste

. . . .

Preheat oven to 375°.

In a small sauté pan, toast the curry powder just until the color changes slightly and the aroma is released. Add the butter and sauté the onion, garlic, mushrooms, pepper and celery until the onion begins to turn clear. Remove from heat folding in the pear, crab and capers.

Mix together the mayonnaise, lemon zest, citrus rum, egg, breadcrumbs, pepper and salt. Fold in the crab mixture. Turn this into a buttered glass baking dish.

Bake for 20 minutes and serve hot with crisp crackers or buttered toast points.

Spices will retain their peak flavor much longer if stored in glass containers. Plastic tends to absorb the volatile oils of the spices making them old before their time.

RUM COCONUT SHRIMP

Grenada

YIELD: 24 appetizers

Even though I don't consume much fat, I have always loved this classic tropical recipe for deep fried shrimp. The unique dipping sauce that follows also came from Grenada, found on one of our many explorations.

24	*jumbo shrimp, shelled and deveined*
1	*large beaten egg*
2	*tablespoons coconut rum*
1	*clove garlic, minced*
½	*teaspoon sea salt*
½	*teaspoon pepper*
¾	*cup of plain breadcrumbs*
1	*cup shredded coconut, fresh or from the package*
	vegetable oil for deep frying

. . . .

Arrange three separate bowls as follows: one for the breadcrumbs, sea salt and pepper, one for the egg, garlic and rum, and the last for the coconut. Start heating the oil in the deep fryer.

Rinse the shrimp under cold water and pat dry. Dredge in the breadcrumb mixture. Dip in the egg and then roll in the coconut.

Drop the shrimp a few at a time in the heated oil, frying until golden. Drain on plain white paper towels, absorbing as much oil as possible. Serve with Spicy Equatorial Sauce.

SPICY EQUATORIAL SAUCE

Grenada

YIELD: about 1 cup

I always like to have several different types of chutneys on hand. These can be used as the base in numerous recipes, sauces, spreads and dips. This is a good way to experiment with those different flavored rums as well.

¾	*cup of Mango-Passion Chutney*
4	*tablespoons Mango Rum*
2	*tablespoons Dijon-style mustard*
1	*teaspoon lime zest*
	juice of ½ a lime
1	*teaspoon Junkanoo Hot Sauce*

. . . .

Mix all ingredients in a small glass bowl. Allow to refrigerate overnight to set the flavors. Serve with Rum Coconut Shrimp or fritters.

GUAVABERRY RUM TENDERS

St. Martin

YIELD: 24 appetizers

Sing along with us, "Good morning, good morning, I come from a guavaberry". I remember my island-born husband singing this to myself and the children, coaxing us to wake up. Guavaberry liqueur is made on the island of St. Martin or St. Maarten (Dutch spelling). Double this recipe as these delectable guavaberry-raspberry wings will be sure to go quickly. Good variations of this recipe can be had by using chutney, but be sure to purée in the blender or food processor first.

2½ - 3	pounds of chicken wings	½	teaspoon lime zest
½	cup raspberry preserves	¼	cup chicken stock
1	tablespoon orange marmalade	¼	cup minced yellow onion
3	tablespoons guavaberry liqueur	1	tablespoon minced garlic
3	tablespoons dark rum juice of one lime	½	teaspoon Junkanoo Hot Sauce
		¼	teaspoon ground cinnamon salt and pepper

. . . .

Preheat oven to 350°.

Whirl all ingredients except the chicken, salt and pepper in the blender until absolutely smooth.

In a glass baking dish, arrange the chicken wings. Season to taste with salt and pepper. Bake for 20 minutes until chicken is golden and slightly crisp.

In a small sauce pan, heat the preserves until sugar begins to thicken. Pour over the chicken in the glass dish and return to the oven, stirring the chicken occasionally to coat. Bake until the pieces are glazed. Serve while still hot.

FRESH TOMATO SALSA

Antigua

Yield: 6 appetizer servings

The fresh flavors of the basil, olive oil and goat cheese combine well with the tomatoes. The spark comes from the hint of citrus rum. The crunchy toast points go over well as a first course at a luncheon, combining the bread and salad in one appetizer.

1	cup fresh ripe tomatoes, well chopped & allowed to drain	½	tablespoon apple cider vinegar
¼	cup red onion, minced	3	tablespoons mandarin orange sections, drained and chopped
1	clove garlic, minced		
4	tablespoons chopped fresh basil	2	tablespoons olive oil
			dash of Junkanoo Hot Sauce

filling:

1	small package of goat cheese, 4 to 6 ounces
3	tablespoons chopped walnuts
1	tablespoon citrus rum

toast:

one loaf crusty French bread, sliced as thinly as possible
olive oil

. . . .

Sauté the onion and garlic in 1 tablespoon of the olive oil for 3 to 4 minutes. Remove from heat and allow to cool.

In a large glass bowl stir the remaining tablespoon of olive oil with the vinegar and hot sauce. Gently fold in the tomatoes, mandarin orange, basil and cooled onion mixture. Refrigerate at least two hours to marinate.

Mix the goat cheese with the rum and the walnuts and store in the refrigerator.

Preheat the broiler. Brush both sides of the French bread slices with the olive oil. Brown in the broiler, turning each side once.

Spread the goat cheese evenly over the toast. Spoon salsa over the top and arrange artfully on a serving tray.

RUM FETA TART

Aruba

YIELD: 12 appetizer servings

This dish is perfect for those last minute get togethers. It can also be made up to several days ahead of time and actually tastes better with age.

1	store-bought pie crust, baked	2	garlic cloves, minced
1	cup canned plum tomatoes, well drained and chopped	4	ounces of Feta cheese
		½	cup sour cream
2	tablespoons sundried tomatoes packed in oil, chopped	2	eggs, beaten
		¼	cup condensed milk (not sweetened)
2	tablespoons chopped fresh basil	¼	cup grated parmesan cheese
½	cup yellow onion, minced	1	tablespoon olive oil
2	tablespoons gold rum		grated nutmeg

. . . .

Preheat oven to 350°.

Sauté the onion and garlic in the olive oil until just clear. Remove from heat and stir in the rum. In a large glass bowl, gently toss the tomatoes and basil with the onion mixture. Set aside.

In another bowl, cream together the Feta, sour cream and parmesan. Separately combine the beaten egg with the condensed milk.

Layer first the tomatoes then the cheese in alternating layers. Pour eggs over the top. Protect the pie crust edges with the foil and bake for 25 to 30 minutes until slightly golden and firm.

Allow cooling and slice into 12 even pieces. May be served at room temperature or hot. Especially good with fiery Junkanoo Hot Sauce.

CARIBBEAN RUM BALLS
Puerto Rico

YIELD: 6 appetizer servings

No, these are not those luscious chocolately rum balls that are made on St. Thomas. This is a tasty version of that ever-classic standby, Swedish meatballs. Be sure to make plenty ahead of time and use festive toothpicks to spear.

1	pound lean ground beef	1	teaspoon olive oil
¼	pound ground pork	2	tablespoons dark rum
¾	cup seasoned breadcrumbs	¼	teaspoon ground nutmeg
2	cloves garlic	¼	teaspoon ground cinnamon
1	small yellow onion, chopped	1	teaspoon curry powder
		1	egg, beaten
1	small habañero or other hot pepper, minced	1	tablespoon tomato paste
		1	jar pimento stuffed olives

. . . .

Heat oven to 350°.

Heat the spices gently in a small pan, add the olive oil and sauté the garlic, onion and hot pepper. Remove from heat.

In a large heavy bowl, combine the ground beef, pork, and breadcrumbs. In a small bowl, whisk together the egg, tomato paste and the rum. Fold into the meat and form balls the size of a Ping-Pong ball. Stuff the center of each meatball with an olive.

Place meat balls on a metal rack inside of a glass baking dish. This way the excess fat can be drained off and the meatballs will not be soggy. Turn meatballs to allow even browning. Serve with Kiwi Mustard Sauce.

KIWI AND GREEN GRAPE MUSTARD SAUCE

Bonaire

YIELD: about 1 cup

The color of this sauce is particularly pretty. Fill interestingly shaped jars with the sauce (using proper canning procedures), cover with burlap or a bright fabric and tie with raffia for the perfect hostess gift.

2	*medium kiwis, peeled and cubed*
¼	*cup green grapes*
1	*tablespoon Chartreuse*
3	*tablespoons citrus rum*
4	*tablespoons Mango-Passion Chutney*
1	*teaspoon Junkanoo Hot Sauce*
1	*tablespoon Dijon-style mustard*

. . . .

Whirl all ingredients in food processor or blender. Serve with Caribbean Rum Balls or on toast points mixed with goat or cream cheese and walnuts.

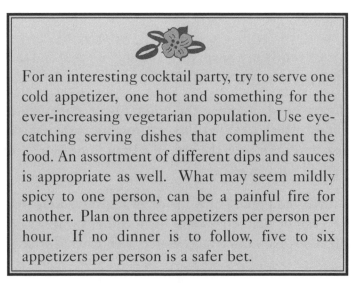

For an interesting cocktail party, try to serve one cold appetizer, one hot and something for the ever-increasing vegetarian population. Use eye-catching serving dishes that compliment the food. An assortment of different dips and sauces is appropriate as well. What may seem mildly spicy to one person, can be a painful fire for another. Plan on three appetizers per person per hour. If no dinner is to follow, five to six appetizers per person is a safer bet.

CHEDDAR MANGO BALLS

Cayman Islands

YIELD: approximately 2½ cups

This is another one of those lifesaving last minute, pull it out of a hat appetizers that makes your culinary skills look really good. Serve with a good assortment of crisp crackers, cut up pears, apples, celery and a good Chardonnay. Yes, you can mix the small amount of rum in the cheese with white wine without any disastrous results!

8	*ounces of cream cheese at room temperature*
8	*ounces of extra sharp aged cheddar cheese, grated*
¼	*cup of sour cream*
¼	*cup Mango-Passion Chutney*
3	*tablespoons pineapple rum*
1	*teaspoon Junkanoo Hot Sauce*
¾	*cup crushed walnuts*

. . . .

Blend all the ingredients in a food processor except walnuts. With greased hands, form into a large ball and roll in the crushed walnuts.

Refrigerate overnight
or until firm.

CURRIED SHRIMP ROTI

Trinidad

YIELD: 8 Roti

If I were allowed only one food, it would be roti. The filling variations are endless, sure to please meat eaters and vegetarians alike. Many years ago, we hired a Trinidadian housekeeper that made us roti once a week, along with fresh, homemade chutney from local mangos. Unfortunately, the lady became ill and I will never forget the look on my husband's face when the end of the roti was announced.

wraps:

2¼ cups all-purpose flour (unbleached flour may be substituted successfully)	¼ teaspoon nutmeg dash of hot pepper sauce
½ teaspoon baking soda	5 tablespoons condensed milk (not sweetened)
¼ teaspoon salt	clarified butter to fry

filling:

1 pound medium shrimp, shelled and deveined	¾ cup cubed potato (very tasty with the skin left on)
¼ cup yellow onion, minced	1 tablespoon vegetable oil
2 cloves garlic, minced	1 tablespoon curry powder
1 small red bell pepper, seeded and minced	3 tablespoons fresh or canned pineapple, finely diced
½ teaspoon fresh grated ginger	1 tablespoon pineapple rum
	1 cup fish or chicken broth

. . . .

Make the filling first by heating the curry powder until the aroma is released in a medium skillet. Add the vegetable oil and sauté the onion, garlic, pepper, potato, pineapple and ginger for ten minutes. Remove from heat.

In a small pot heat the broth and plunge in the shrimp, simmering over low heat for 15 minutes. Drain the shrimp and mix with the onions and rum. Set aside.

In the meanwhile sift the dry ingredients for the wraps into a large bowl. Add the milk and knead the resulting dough for two to three minutes. Transfer to a lightly floured board. Divide the dough into eight equal pieces. Let sit for 10 minutes. Use a floured rolling pin and roll out each ball. Allow to sit for another 20 minutes and roll out again, thinly. Heat a non-stick pan and lightly brown each roti until golden.

Fill each roti with curried shrimp filling and roll up. Serve with Junkanoo Hot Sauce and Mango-Passion Chutney.

BROCCOLI AND CITRUS RUM ROTI

Trinidad

YIELD: 8 rotis

This dish will sate the appetite of vegetarians and everyone in between. I like to serve this with copious amounts of chutney and hot sauce, with a little Rum Fried Plantain on the side.

1	cup fresh broccoli florets, well chopped and lightly steamed until just tender	¼	cup yellow onion, minced
		3	cloves garlic, minced
½	cup garbanzo beans, either fresh or from can and drained	1	tablespoon fresh grated ginger
		1½	tablespoons curry powder
¼	cup canned plum tomatoes, drained and chopped		zest of one lemon
			juice of one lemon
½	cup cubed boiled potato	1	tablespoon citrus rum
		2	tablespoons clarified butter

. . . .

Gently heat the curry powder until the color changes and a pleasant aroma is given off. Add the clarified butter and sauté the onion, garlic, and ginger. Remove from heat.

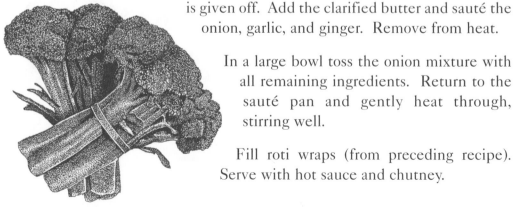

In a large bowl toss the onion mixture with all remaining ingredients. Return to the sauté pan and gently heat through, stirring well.

Fill roti wraps (from preceding recipe). Serve with hot sauce and chutney.

PUMPKIN APPLE FRITTERS

Curacao

Yield: appetizers for 6 to 8

Serve these fritters for breakfast when you have weekend houseguests. High in vitamin A, they make for a nutritious and elegant breakfast.

¾	*pound fresh pumpkin, cubed*	2	*egg yolks*
1	*peeled cored apple, cubed*	1	*large egg, beaten*
4	*tablespoons flour*		*plain breadcrumbs*
¼	*teaspoon cinnamon*	6	*tablespoons coconut*
¼	*teaspoon nutmeg*		*shredded coconut*
¼	*cup brown sugar*		*oil for frying*

. . . .

Boil the pumpkin and apple until just tender. Remove from heat, drain and mash the pumpkin. Set the apples aside.

In a large glass bowl, combine the flour, spices and sugar. Add the egg yolks, pumpkin and coconut, mixing well. Shape into small balls the size of a Ping-Pong, dip in the beaten egg. Roll in the breadcrumbs, then the coconut.

Deep fry until golden. Drain on white paper towels and dust with brown sugar.

Serve at once.

LEMON CONCH CAKES

St. Croix

YIELD: 8 appetizer servings

This is a delightful variation of the perennial favorite, crab cakes. Adjust the fire to your taste and serve with Avocado Butter.

1 pound conch meat, cleaned and pounded	1 teaspoon lemon zest
6 eggs	2 teaspoons fresh thyme leaves, chopped
½ cup white cornmeal	2 tablespoons fresh parsley, chopped
½ cup unbleached white flour	
½ small serrano or other fiery pepper, seeded and minced	4 tablespoons light rum
1 celery stalk, finely chopped	1 tablespoon Tabasco® pepper sauce
1 small yellow onion, minced	cracker crumbs
2 cloves garlic, minced	safflower oil for frying
juice of one lemon	salt and pepper to taste

. . . .

Put the conch through the food processor or meat grinder. Combine all ingredients except cracker crumbs and safflower oil in a large bowl.

Form into patties and roll in cracker crumbs. Fry in hot oil until golden. Drain on white paper towels. Season with salt and pepper, serve with Avocado Butter.

AVOCADO BUTTER

Bahamas

YIELD: About 1 cup

I like to use this creamy sauce on everything from seafood to chicken to pasta. The lemon juice in the recipe will keep the avocado from turning brown too quickly.

1	*stick butter at room temperature*
½	*ripe avocado*
1	*tablespoon lemon juice*
1	*tablespoon light rum*
½	*teaspoon fresh grated ginger*
2	*teaspoons tamari sauce*

. . . .

Chop the avocado well and cream in a small bowl. Beat in the butter gradually. Add all other ingredients. Serve a dollop on Lemon Conch Cakes.

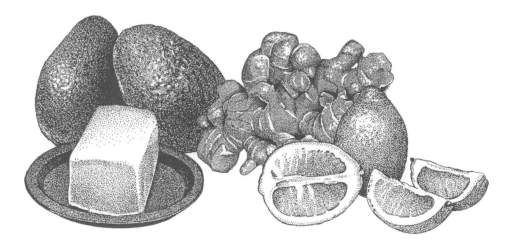

ORANGE GARLIC LOBSTER BALLS

Anguilla

YIELD: 6 to 8 appetizer servings

Anguilla is a beautiful island filled with beaches and lovely coral reefs. Each beach is different on the island; some are long deserted stretches, and others filled with bars and activity, some with wild surf, others with dunes.

The heady sweetness of the orange combines well with the piquancy of the garlic.

Besides serving with the following sauce, keep a little hot sauce on hand for those who like more fire.

2	medium lobster tails	1	teaspoon fresh cilantro, chopped
¼	cup butter, softened	1	tablespoon orange juice concentrate
½	cup breadcrumbs		
¼	cup shallots	1	teaspoon orange zest
1	teaspoon fresh grated ginger	2	tablespoons dark rum
1	clove garlic, crushed		oil for frying

. . . .

Chop the lobster tail finely and combine with all other ingredients except oil in a large heavy bowl. Form into small balls the size of a walnut.

Heat the oil and fry two or three balls at a time until golden. Serve with Passionfruit Rum Glaze.

PASSIONFRUIT RUM GLAZE

British Virgin Islands

YIELD: approximately 1½ cups

*C*ombine this glaze with a little homemade barbecue sauce for the perfect marinade for pork chops or spareribs. Works equally well over vanilla ice cream or lime sorbet.

5	*fresh passionfruit or ½ cup frozen concentrate*
¼	*teaspoon fresh grated ginger*
¾	*cup of water*
¼	*cup citrus rum*
¼	*cup brown sugar*
1¼	*teaspoons cornstarch*
	dash of ground cinnamon

Peel and seed the passionfruit. Whirl in a blender with the rum, ginger and cinnamon until smooth. In a small saucepan, mix water, brown sugar and cornstarch. Over medium heat bring to a boil, stirring constantly until barely thickened.

Stir in the passionfruit and gently cook for one minute. Remove from heat and allow to cool.

SALMON LIME DIP

St. Barths

Yield: nearly 2 cups

*H*ere's another one of those quick yet impressive recipes for surprise company. Keep a couple of cans of salmon on hand as well as hard-boiled eggs.

1	*12-ounce can of pink salmon*		*juice of ½ a lime*
¼	*cup minced red onion*	2	*tablespoons mayonnaise*
2	*hard-boiled eggs, chopped*	1	*teaspoon fresh tarragon,*
2	*tablespoons light rum*		*chopped*

· · · · · · · · · ·

Open can of salmon, drain and press out any excess water carefully. In a small bowl combine all other ingredients.

Serve with pepper crackers.

COCONUT CRAB PUFFS

Bermuda

YIELD: 8 to 10 appetizer servings

*B*ermuda really is not a Caribbean island. But for some reason, I tend to think of it so. Besides, this recipe came from my Bermudan friend that lived on St. Thomas for many years following Hurricane Hugo.

2 or 3   sheets puff pastry

1 *cup cream cheese*	2	*tablespoons coconut*
1 *cup fresh or canned crabmeat*		*dash of ground cinnamon & nutmeg*
5 *tablespoons sweetened grated*		*oil for frying*
coconut		

· · · · · · · · · ·

Mix all ingredients together except for the puff pastry. Wrap small spoonfuls in the puff pastry and drop into the hot oil. Fry until golden.

Drain on white paper towels. Serve with Mango-Horseradish Sauce.

MANGO-HORSERADISH SAUCE

Turks

YIELD: 1 cup

This sauce will keep for several weeks in the refrigerator. I also like to add a splash of fiery hot sauce to heat things up.

¾	*cup Mango-Passion Chutney*
¼	*cup horseradish*
2	*tablespoons lime rum*
½	*teaspoon fresh grated lime zest*
	dash of ground anise

. . . .

In a small glass bowl, whisk together all the ingredients including the ground anise.

Serve with Coconut Crab Puffs, fritters, chicken or fish. It's also great on sandwiches made with stone ground bread, cream cheese, spinach, raspberries and onions.

CALYPSO SALSA

St. John

YIELD: Approximately 3½ cups

I really like this recipe as it is colorful, bursting with flavor, and quite low in fat. Serve with an assortment of chips such as blue corn or the new spicy low fat kind.

1	cup chopped tomatoes	½	teaspoon cumin
½	cup corn kernels (frozen or canned)	3	tablespoons lime rum
		2	tablespoons fresh lime juice
½	cucumber, peeled and well chopped	¼	cup cilantro leaves, chopped
1	bell pepper, seeded and chopped	¼	cup finely chopped walnuts
½	scotch bonnet pepper	3	tablespoons olive oil
1	small yellow onion, minced		dash of freshly grated ginger
4	cloves garlic, crushed		sea salt and ground pepper to taste
1	ripe avocado, chopped		

. . . .

Fold all ingredients together in a large heavy bowl. If not to be served immediately, add a little extra lime juice to keep the avocado from turning color.

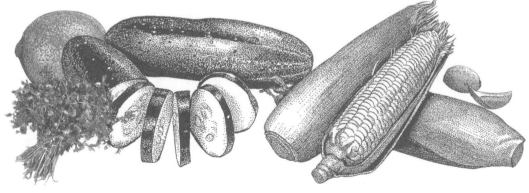

PORK-PINEAPPLE BITES

Jamaica

YIELD: 6 to 8 appetizer servings

The use of fresh fruit in this jerk recipe adds a wonderful luscious flavor to the meat. Compare this jerk recipe from Jamaica to the following one from Puerto Rico, using pork as well. It's funny how islands relatively close in proximity can have such vast historical culinary differences.

2	*pounds boneless pork loin cubed*
1	*small onion, finely chopped*
½	*cup fresh pineapple, chopped*
2	*teaspoons fresh thyme leaves*
4	*cloves garlic*
2	*scotch bonnet peppers, seeded and minced*
1	*teaspoon freshly ground pepper*
1	*teaspoon allspice*
¼	*teaspoon nutmeg*
½	*teaspoon cinnamon*
2	*tablespoons olive oil*
1	*teaspoon tamari sauce*
2	*tablespoons dark rum*

. . . .

In a food processor blend the onion, pineapple, thyme, garlic, peppers and all other ingredients except the pork. Purée until a paste forms.

In a large ziplock bag, toss the pork cubes and jerk marinade. Refrigerate overnight.

Heat the grill to a low, even temperature. Meat cooks best this way. Cook very slowly for at least one hour. Serve skewered with fancy toothpicks.

ADOBO RUM PORK CUBES

Puerto Rico

YIELD: 6 to 8 appetizer servings

Adobo is a basic seasoning in Puerto Rico. This condiment is a combination of spices that keeps very well. Keep in the refrigerator to extend the shelf life. Use for rubbing meat, chicken and seafood. Also use as a soup base and as a seasoning for pastas, vegetables and rice dishes. Traditionally, a mortar and pestle is used in this recipe to crush and pound the ingredients. I highly recommend the use of one for true authenticity.

1	*tablespoon kosher salt*
½	*teaspoon ground cumin*
½	*teaspoon coriander*
1	*teaspoon paprika*
½	*tablespoon coarsely ground fresh pepper*
3	*cloves garlic, minced*
1	*tablespoon chopped oregano*
1	*tablespoon chopped cilantro*
½	*teaspoon freshly grated ginger*
1	*tablespoon light rum*
2	*pounds boneless pork loin cubes*

. . . .

In a mortar and pestle, crush and pound all the ingredients except the pork. Continue until a paste forms.

In a large re-sealable plastic bag, toss the pork cubes and the Adobo. Marinate in the refrigerator overnight.

Heat the grill to low-to-medium heat and barbecue the pork. Check for tenderness in 45 minutes to an hour. Serve with toothpicks and Mojito Rum Sauce.

MOJITO RUM SAUCE

Puerto Rico

YIELD: approximately 2½ cups

Mojito is the most popular sauce in Puerto Rico. Traditionally it is a sauce for seafood and indeed it is most wonderful over freshly fried crisp fish. The ingredients are a bit difficult to find, so some substitutions will have to be made. While in a Hispanic grocery do look for the culantro leaf and the sweet cherry peppers. If culantro cannot be found, use cilantro.

½	cup olive oil
6	cloves garlic, crushed
½	cup red onion, minced
1	habañero pepper, seeded and minced
1	cup chopped fresh ripe tomatoes
2	tablespoons tomato purée
½	small green bell pepper, seeded and minced
½	small red bell pepper, seeded and minced
¼	cup fresh culantro or cilantro, chopped
¼	cup light rum
½	teaspoon lemon zest
2	tablespoons lime juice.

. . . .

In a large skillet, sauté the olive oil, garlic, red onion, and peppers. Over low heat, cook the onions until clear. Add the rum and swish around the pan. Stir in all remaining ingredients and bring to a low simmer. Cook for 5 more minutes.

Serve over seafood, meat and poultry dishes.

PINEAPPLE RUM PHULOURI

Trinidadi

YIELD: appetizers for 8 to 10

Even though this is an ideal dish for vegetarians, meat lovers will like this as well. Serve with a spicy chutney or hot pepper sauce..

½   cup garbanzo beans,
         cooked or canned and drained
½   cup cooked split peas
½   small onion minced
2   cloves garlic minced
1   tablespoon pineapple rum
1   teaspoon hot sauce
         dash of freshly grated ginger
         sea salt and fresh ground pepper to taste
         safflower oil

. . . .

Heat one tablespoon of the oil and sauté the onions, garlic and ginger. Remove from heat. In a food processor or blender purée all the ingredients.

Heat the oil in a pan with deep sides. Form the purée into small balls and deep fry until golden. Drain on white paper towels. Serve on toothpicks as an appetizer.

SPICE ISLAND GUNDY

Jamaica

YIELD: 2 cups

This recipe is primarily Jamaican, even though you can find it in the French islands and the U. S. Virgin Islands. Perfect for parties, make this several days ahead of time.

1	pound pickled herring
½	cup cooked chicken or steak
¼	cup white vinegar
¼	cup white minced onion
1	clove garlic, minced
1	teaspoon ground allspice
½	cup chopped steamed carrot
½	cup chopped steamed broccoli
¼	cup chopped celery
2	tablespoons capers
1	hard boiled egg, chopped
¼	cup safflower oil
	salt and pepper to taste

. . . .

In a small sauce pan, heat the vinegar and allspice, bringing to a boil. Remove from heat and set side.

In a large glass baking dish, arrange all other ingredients. Pour the vinegar over the top of this and refrigerate overnight. Remove from refrigerator, stir thoroughly and mash.

Serve as a spread for crackers or as a dip for raw vegetables.

RUM SALMON

Curacao

YIELD: 10 to 12 appetizer servings

The cuisine of Curacao has a strong Spanish influence like that of Puerto Rico. Do not plan this salad at the last minute as extra preparation time is required. Be sure to serve with plain toast points or water crackers.

2	pounds cooked salmon, chopped
1	large red onion, chopped
1	scotch bonnet pepper, seeded and minced
3	cloves garlic
1	bay leaf
4	cloves
1	tablespoon capers
¼	cup canned beets, drained
1	tablespoon olive oil
¾	cup apple cider vinegar

. . . .

Sauté the onion, pepper, and garlic in the oil until just barely cooked.

Combine all other ingredients with the onion mixture in a large glass baking dish. Mix well and marinate overnight in the refrigerator.

Remove from refrigerator, mash somewhat and serve at once.

RUM DRINKS
an Introduction

Rum is considered preferred over other hard liquors such as gin, vodka or whiskey because there is sugar already present in the cane and therefore the rum does not need to go through a malting process. For mixing with fruit juices, sodas and in frozen drinks such as pina colada, purchase inexpensive white or dark rum. The darker the rum, the sweeter it is. Save the special reserve and estate blends to drink neat, on the rocks, or with a splash of soda.

This book is meant to have fun with. So put on a little Caribbean music, whip out the blender and shaker and above all, experiment! I have to admit I did more than my share of experimenting when I wrote this book. Don't tell anyone, but half the drink recipes were written after I proofed some of the results, as well as some of the appetizer recipes.

You will find recipes for your basic piña colada and banana daiquiri, to souped-up versions of the same and all other sorts of traditional and non-traditional Caribbean drinks. Some are tame, some are not. Try and find some of the prettiest glasses you can find to serve these drinks. Tall frosted tulip shaped ones are ideal for fruit drinks and blender drinks. Be adventuresome with garnishes, slices of citrus, pineapple, small umbrellas, stirrers in the shape of a palm tree or flamingo or even hibiscus flowers.

Let's take a trip to paradise!

DRINKS

ANGEL'S HELL

British Virgin Islands

1   ounce Pusser's Rum
1   ounce créme de cassis
1   ounce blue curacao
1   ounce light cream

The British Virgin Islands are considered the sailing capitAl of the Caribbean. Even though they are just a few miles from their sister islands, the U. S. Virgin Islands, they have remained relatively unspoiled and undeveloped.

Layer this drink as follows: Créme de Cassis (hell), rum (purgatory), blue curacao (gates of heaven) cream (heaven). Voila!

ANGUILLAN DEVIL

Anguilla

. . . .

1   ounce dark Rum
1   ounce grenadine
1   ounce pineapple Juice
     juice of one lemon
     fresh pineapple slices

Anguilla is located halfway down the Caribbean chain, with the island's main attraction being its scores of beaches. This island is the farthest north of the Leeward Islands, resting in both the Caribbean and Atlantic Ocean.

Shake all ingredients well and serve in a frosted glass over crushed ice.

AUNT MARY

. . . .

1   ounce coconut rum
1   ounce chocolate liqueur
    chocolate shavings
1   ounce light cream
    short splash of triple sec

St. Martin/St. Maarten has both a Dutch and French side. Each side has its own unique personality.

Use an ice shaker for this one and strain into a rocks glass. Dust with chocolate shavings.

BAHAMA MAMA

Nassau

. . . .

1   ounce rum
1   ounce cherry brandy
2   ounces pineapple juice
2   ounces orange juice
    juice of ½ lemon
1   teaspoon powdered sugar
    crushed ice

Nassau has an enormous cruise ship and hotel industry. We went there for a convention recently and were pleasantly surprised with the hospitality and professionalism shown us. The island is just a short hop from Miami, imparts Caribbean flair without the long hours of travel and changing planes.

Shake all ingredients well and serve in a frosted glass over crushed ice.

BERMUDA SUNSET

Bermuda

. . . .

1	ounce grenadine
1	ounce orange Juice
1	ounce gold rum
1	ounce champagne

See if you can find a margarita glass for this one, as the layers are especially attractive.

Pour the ingredients in the order listed, being careful not to disturb each layer.

BANANA BOAT

St. Lucia

. . . .

2	ounces coconut rum
2	ounces milk
½	ripe banana
	crushed ice

St. Lucia is a stunningly beautiful island consisting of two huge mountains called the Pitons rising to 2,400 feet in height, located in the Windward Islands. Whirl all ingredients in the blender until smooth.

BANANA DAIQUIRI
St. Thomas

. . . .

1   large ripe banana
2   ounces dark rum
      splash of Triple Sec
      juice of one lime
1   ounce light cream
      crushed ice

This is supposedly the original banana daiquiri recipe, and I suppose it may well be as it is the most basic that I have come across. These are quite addicting, which is all fine and dandy, but oh, the calories!

In a blender, pour in the liquid ingredients first, then add the banana, broken up. Once puréed smooth, add small amounts of ice until the desired consistency is reached.

BANANAQUIT
Martinique

. . . .

1   ounce Galliano liqueur
1   ounce light rum
1   ounce orange juice
1   ounce light cream
      crushed ice

The extinct Arawak Indians named the island of Martinique Madinina, which translates to Island of Flowers. Martinique is two-thirds down the island chain, just past Dominica and slightly larger. The island is replete with lush tropical fauna, mountains, rainforest and sunken treasure just waiting to be discovered.

In a shaker combine all ingredients well. Serve either straight up or over the crushed ice.

BEACHED SAILOR

Cayman Islands

. . . .

1	ounce light rum
½	ounce apricot brandy
½	teaspoon Rose's lime juice
2	ounces light cream

Columbus named these islands Las Tortugas when he noticed all the turtle swimming around the islands. The Caymans with their caves and coves are replete with tales of piracy. Only some 480 miles south of Miami, and close to Jamaica, it is one of the most popular destinations in the eastern Caribbean.

Pour all the ingredients over ice in a rocks glass and stir gently.

BETWEEN THE SHEETS

Guadeloupe

. . . .

1	ounce citrus rum
½	ounce cognac
½	ounce Cointreau
	orange peel twist

French is the official language in Guadeloupe and sugar is the principal source of revenue for this laid back island. Located between Antigua and Dominica in the Leeward Islands Guadeloupe is more like a collection of islands, with two main ones connected by a drawbridge, Basse-Terre and Grande-Terre.

Mix all liquid ingredients pour over ice. Garnish with the orange peel twist.

BIG BAMBOO
St. Thomas

. . . .

1   ounce Cruzan Rum
1   ounce citrus rum
1   ounce Grand Marnier
     juice of one lime
     lime zest

Using a drink shaker, shake all ingredients vigorously and garnish with a sprinkle of lime zest.

By the way, my husband named this drink. Any questions, our address is located in the front of this book. His name is Richard.

BLUE BAY
Curacao

. . . .

½   ounce Blue Curacao
1½   ounces lemon rum
     juice of one lemon
½   ounce simple syrup
2   ounces water
     crushed ice

Curacao is the largest island in the Netherland Antilles, located approximately 35 miles north of Venezuela. One of the most impressive beaches on the island is called Blauwbaai or Blue Bay.

Shake all ingredients well in a shaker with crushed ice. Pour into a tall glass.

BOCA CHICA SHOOTER
Dominican Republic

. . . .

½ ounce Frangelico
1 ounce gold rum
½ ounce orange juice

The Dominican Republic takes up two-thirds of the island of Hispaniola. Hispaniola is the large island closest to Cuba. Columbus happened upon the island in December, 1492, when his ship the Santa Maria wrecked.

Shake all ingredients and pour straight up into a shooter.

BROWN-EYED GIRL
Puerto Rico

. . . .

1 ounce dark rum
1 ounce Kahlua
1 ounce Bailey's Irish Cream liqueur
1 ounce light cream

Puerto Rico is a huge (110 miles by 35) diversified island. From El Yunque, its 28,000-acre rainforest, hundreds of beaches and Spanish architecture, there is something for everyone. I really love Old San Juan with its cobblestone streets, charming hideaway restaurants and stone walls.

Using a shaker with a strainer fitted over the top, fill with ice and the dark rum and Kahlua. Shake and strain into a rocks glass. Carefully pour first the Bailey's, then the cream.

BUCCANEER'S BREW

St. Kitts

. . . .

1½ ounces dark rum
1   tablespoon grenadine
6   ounces cola
     lime slice

This drink has always reminded me of the cherry cokes I loved as a kid. While cruising down-island, we came across this tiny bar on the island of St. Kitts. The island is about 65 square miles, but not short on verdant beauty. It is lush, mountainous, complete with rainforests and dazzling waterfalls.

Gently stir all ingredients and pour into a tall glass over ice. Squeeze the lime slice into the drink and toss in.

BUSHWHACKER

Antigua

. . . .

1   ounce dark rum
1   ounce coconut rum
1   ounce chocolate liqueur
1   ounce Bailey's Irish
     Cream liqueur
     crushed ice
     nutmeg

Grinding your own fresh nutmeg really is the best bet for these recipes. This drink is really filling and best suited to Sunday afternoons by the pool when you may consider drinking your lunch.

Fill a blender with slightly less than 1 cup of crushed ice. Add all ingredients except the nutmeg and blend until an ice cream consistency is attained. Sprinkle with ground nutmeg.

CARNIVAL JUMP UP

St. Croix

. . . .

1   ounce banana rum
1   ounce coconut rum
2   tablespoons simple syrup
     juice of one lime
     lime zest

St. Croix holds its annual carnival during the first week of January, extending the merry holiday season delightfully. While more laid back than St. Thomas, it is equally beautiful. History buffs will revel in the ancient Danish architecture and the best-preserved fort in the Caribbean. The island has lush, gently sloping hills and miles of secluded beaches.

Shake all ingredients vigorously and pour into a tall glass filled with ice cubes. Garnish with a few sprinkles of lime zest.

CHOCOCO

St. Eustatius

. . . .

1   ounce light rum
1   ounce chocolate liqueur
½   ounce coconut rum
1   banana
2   ounces light cream
     dusting of nutmeg
     crushed ice

This Dutch island is pronounced STAY-sha and is 35 miles south of St. Martin. The airplane landing on Statia is quite an event in itself. One flies directly over an extinct volcano complete with a verdant tropical rainforest in its center. This tiny island is only 12 miles square and has remained a Dutch possession since 1816.

Combine all ingredients except the nutmeg in the blender. Pour into a tall tulip-shaped glass and sprinkle with nutmeg.

CHOCOLATE KISS

St. Thomas

. . . .

1½	ounces dark rum
2	ounces Hershey's Syrup
4	ounces of milk
	splash of Amaretto

My 12-year old daughter called me at work one afternoon and informed me of this new drink she made up for Just Add Rum. Roxanne has always been a very helpful child and I must say it tasted quite delicious once I added the alcohol to it.

According to Roxanne, toss all ingredients into the blender with seven ice cubes. Pour into a tulip-shaped glass, allow to sit for one minute until the layers begin to separate nicely.

EL COQUI

Puerto Rico

. . . .

1	ounce Midori
1	ounce white rum
	juice of one lime
	fresh zest of lime
4	ounces orange juice

Now, if you've traveled to Puerto Rico, you may be under the incorrect impression that the Coqui frog is green. Oh, before I continue, the Coqui is a tiny treefrog who is found only in Puerto Rico that has attained tremendous popularity. His nightly song is kokee, kokee, which can also become quite deafening. At any rate, souvenir shops have depicted this happy-go-lucky creature as a bright lime green. He is not green, more like a golden tan, hence the orange juice in this drink tempers the green of the Midori. Here, here for accuracy.

Pour all ingredients except the lime zest into a tall glass. Using a long stirrer, blend all ingredients well until a pale mud-like color is achieved. Sprinkle sparingly with lime zest.

CREAMSICLE

St. Thomas

. . . .

1   ounce Galliano liqueur
½   ounce Grand Marnier
1   ounce light rum
2   ounces milk
     slice of fresh orange

St. Thomas has one of the world's ten most beautiful beaches, Magen's Bay. Palm-rimmed, mile-long Magen's Bay also has a fabulous bar where years ago I had this luscious yet potent drink. This is my version of it.

Fill a drink shaker with ice and all ingredients except for the orange slice. Shake vigorously and pour into a tall glass. Garnish with a slice of orange.

DREAM MAKER

Grenadines

. . . .

1   ounce Rum Cream
     Liqueur
1   ounce Tia Maria
1   ounce Galliano
2   ounces orange juice
     crushed ice

The Grenadines and St. Vincent are lush volcanic islands located in the Windward Islands. The beaches on St. Vincent are a beautiful black compared to the Grenadines sparkling white beaches.

Stir well and serve over crushed ice.

FRANGIPANI
Trinidad

. . . .

1 ounce mango rum
1 ounce Cointreau
1 ounce half and half
3 ounces frozen strawberries
   crushed ice

Trinidad is a huge island with many exports including gorgeous tropical flowers of all types. The island is home to more than 400 species of birds and twice that many orchids.

Whirl all ingredients in the blender and serve in a pretty tulip-shaped glass.

GIRL SCOUT COOKIE
St. Thomas

. . . .

1 ounce light rum
1 ounce white crème de menthe
1 ounce dark crème de cacao
1 ounce light cream

I really like this drink, especially at the beach on Sunday afternoons. It also makes a good frozen drink, different from the regular fruit base concoctions.

Shake all ingredients well and serve over crushed ice.

HIBISCUS

Barbados

. . . .

2   ounces cranberry juice
2   ounces champagne
1   ounce light rum
     crushed ice

Say the word hibiscus and immediately an image of a brilliant red tropical flower come up. Did you know that hibiscus come in all shades ranging from white, bubble gum pink, orange, blue and yes, even brown? Some appear like hippie tie-dyed tee shirts with a deep blue center, brown middle and red edges. I'm sure you can tell by now that this is my favorite flower. We have dozens of varieties in our yard and my long-suffering husband is constantly kept busy repotting and transplanting them for me.

Fill a drink shaker with ice and all the ingredients except the champagne. Shake well and strain into a tall glass. Gradually and carefully stir in the champagne. Garnish with a hibiscus flower if you have as they are not poisonous.

IGUANA

St. Thomas

. . . .

1   ounce citrus or lime rum
1   ounce coconut rum
1   ounce Coco Lopez
     crushed ice
1   tablespoon fresh lime juice
     slice of lime

What was formerly known as Limetree Beach Hotel on St. Thomas was a familiar stomping ground for these gentle lizards. Attaining 4 feet or more in length, they are herbivores and more than a little shy, or so I was told. When I first moved to the islands, I spent a great deal of time at the beaches and local hotel pools. No one bothered to tell me that iguanas are very attracted to bright red colors. I suppose because that means lunch to them, i.e. hibiscus. Much to my dismay, while dozing, I had my foot nudged by one of these Kamota dragon look-a-likes. He had discovered my red toe nail polish!

Whirl all the ingredients in a blender and garnish with a lime slice. Very cool and refreshing.

ISLAND CHAMPAGNE

St. John, U. S. Virgin Islands

. . . .

½   ounce banana rum
½   ounce mango rum
     champagne
     mango slice

This is St. John, U. S. Virgin Islands, not St. Johns, Antigua. St. John is only a pleasant 20-minute ferry ride from St. Thomas' East End. Most of the island is National Park and quite unspoiled. Expect mountainous, hairpin roads and darling donkeys on your way to some of the most beautiful beaches in the Caribbean.

In a champagne glass, first pour in the banana rum, then mango rum. Fill to the top with chilled champagne and garnish with a mango slice.

JUMP UP & KISS ME

Saba

. . . .

1   ounce dark rum
1   ounce mango rum
     juice of one lime
     splash of pineapple juice

The island of Saba is only five square miles with a population of approximately 1200 inhabitants. There are no beaches to speak of on the island as steep volcanic cliffs surround it. The capital is called The Bottom and it is at the top of the hill rather than the bottom as one would expect. Saba is probably the most enchanting island in the Caribbean with its gingerbread houses and neat picket fences with flowers tumbling over the top. Just a quick 15-minute flight from St. Maarten, this island is ideal for the person who truly wants to get away.

Shake all ingredients and pour over cracked ice.

KAMIKAZE

St. Thomas

. . . .

1 ounce light rum
¼ ounce Cointreau
  splash of Rose's Lime
  Juice

A friend of mine drinks these shooters and would be appalled to learn that I created a recipe with rum instead of vodka. Actually the rum was so sweet compared to the vodka that I merely adjusted the amount of Cointreau and the result was quite good!

Pour all ingredients into a shooter and sit down and shoot.

KOOL-AID

Turks and Caicos

. . . .

1 ounce mango rum
1 ounce Midori
  juice of one lime
  ginger ale
  ice

The Turks and Caicos consist of eight main islands and approximately 40 islets and cays, with a population of about 14,000. The islands are all relatively untouched and a haven for scuba divers and those who wish peace and privacy.

Shake all ingredients except the ginger ale. Pour the liquor over ice in a tall glass and fill with ginger ale

LIMBO

Dominican Republic

· · · · · · · · · ·

1 ounce dark rum
1 ounce Galliano
1 ounce chocolate liqueur
1 ounce maraschino cherry juice
1 ounce heavy cream chocolate shavings

I didn't know this drink would be so good. It's also really fattening. Maybe that's why they want you to work it off doing the Limbo.

Whirl all ingredients in blender with ½ a cup of crushed ice.

MAI-TAI

Aruba

· · · · · · · · · ·

2 ounces light rum
1 ounce Curacao
½ ounce Amaretto
 juice of ½ a lime
1 ounce simple syrup
1 tablespoon Grenadine

Now, we all know that the Mai-Tai did not originate in Aruba. However when I managed to escape the confines of that cruise ship, I came across this refreshing, yet traditional version of the fabled drink.

Shake with ice and strain into an old-fashioned glass, either straight up or partially filled with cracked ice.

MOCKO JUMBIE

St. Thomas

. . . .

½   ounce coconut rum
½   ounce light rum
1   ounce Midori
2   ounces pineapple juice
     splash of maraschino
     cherry juice

Ok, this is one of the last recipe of the book and I have my very own 11-year old Mocko Jumbie sitting next to me. Now I know how to spell Mocko Jumbie correctly. It has an e at the end. Roxanne is enjoying this immensely as now her name will have to go in the book credits.

Shake all ingredients and pour into a tall glass fill with crushed ice.

PAINKILLER

British Virgin Islands

. . . .

2   ounces 151 proof rum
2   ounces pineapple juice
2   ounces orange juice
     splash of Coco Lopez
     crushed ice
     nutmeg

I had to swim to the bar to get this drink as there is no boat dock at White Bay, Jost Van Dyke. It is quite easy to drink too many of these while swinging on a hammock.

Shake all ingredients well and pour over crushed ice. Garnish with f r e s h l y g r a t e d nutmeg if desired.

PINEAPPLE SPLASH

St. John, U. S. Virgin Islands

. . . .

1½   ounces pineapple rum
½   ounce white crème de
    cacao
    splash of club soda

I happened upon this drink late one afternoon when my secretary and I missed the last car ferry returning from St. John to St. Thomas. I still don't remember exactly when or how we got back, but I did remember the ingredients to this drink.

Shake the rum and crème de cacao and pour over a tumbler of cracked ice. Add a splash of club soda and serve.

PINK BEACH

Bonaire

. . . .

½   ounce Chambord
1   ounce pineapple rum
2   ounces pineapple juice
    splash of cranberry juice
1   ounce half & half

Bonaire is located near to Aruba and Curacao, also quite near to Venezuela. The diving is unparalleled on this rugged desert-like island. Nature lovers will want to go off and explore the abundant natural flora and fauna. Wild flamingos abound as well as a parrot called the Bonairian Lora. Bonaire boasts an underwater marine park developed in coordination with the World Wildlife Fund in 1970. It covers nearly the entire coastline and is protected by stringent environmental laws.

Mix the above ingredients and serve over crushed ice or mix in a blender with ice as a frozen drink.

PLANTER'S PUNCH

Jamaica

. . . .

1½   ounces gold or dark rum
2   ounces simple syrup
       juice of one lime
       one maraschino cherry
       and big splash of juice

Enjoy sipping the national drink of the islands during lazy summer weekends. Orange juice may be substituted for the simple syrup.

Pour all ingredients over ice in a tall glass and stir.

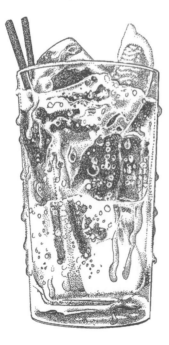

PRINCE RUPERT

Dominica

. . . .

1   ounce Bailey's Irish
     Cream
1   ounce Sambuca
1   ounce rum
2   ounces milk

Prince Rupert Bay is the site of a naval battle in 1782 on the beautiful island of Dominica. This beautiful island claims over two miles of fabulous beaches and tiny hotels.   Located   between Guadeloupe and Martinique, much of this island is covered by rainforest.

In a shaker filled with ice, vigorously shake all ingredients. Pour straight up or over the rocks.

PUERTO RICAN PARROT

Puerto Rico

· · · · · · · ·

1	ounce *Midori*
1	ounce *Galliano*
½	ounce *grenadine*
1	ounce *white rum*

There are only about 40 Puerto Rican parrots left in El Yunque, Puerto Rico's tropical rainforest. These beautiful amazons are on the endangered species list and much loved on the island. I like this drink because the layers are so pretty to look at. You are best off placing the glass in front of your guest or customer, pouring the drink on the spot so as not to mix the colors unduly.

Use a spoon to layer the ingredients into a short tumbler. Fill halfway full of ice and first pour in the grenadine syrup. Using the spoon, pour the Midori over the bowl of the spoon slowly so as to not disturb the grenadine underneath. Do the same for the Galliano and float the white rum on the top.

SAN JUAN COFFEE

Puerto Rico

. . . .

1	*ounce coffee liqueur*
2	*ounces gold rum*
	splash of Crème de Noyaux
	splash of Galliano
	strong hot coffee
	nutmeg

San Juan is a glittering city in the Caribbean complete with high-rises, luxury resort, casino and miles of beach, much like Miami. Yet, close by is charming Old San Juan with its centuries old fortresses and cobblestone streets. Puerto Rico, 110 miles long and 35 miles wide, is a diversified island bursting with Spanish history and architecture, a 28,000 acres of tropical rainforest, thousands of miles of beaches, mountains, rivers, underground grottos and dry tropical forest. This island surely will please the most sophisticated traveler.

In a tall ceramic coffee cup combine all the liqueur and gradually stir in the piping hot coffee. Garnish with a grating of fresh nutmeg.

SCUBA ARUBA

Aruba

. . . .

1   ounce Blue Curacao
1   ounce lime rum
1   ounce light rum
     7-up
     lime wedge

Aruba's waters have visibility up to 90 feet making it excellent for snorkeling or scuba diving. Aruba is located way down in the Lesser Antilles close to Venezuela, South America. There is one main strip that is home to nearly all the major hotels, restaurants, night clubs and shopping. The beaches are gorgeous and unspoiled.

Fill a tall glass with ice and stir in the liquor. Fill to the top with 7-up and stir gently. Garnish with a lime wedge.

SEX ON THE BEACH

Grenada

. . . .

½   ounce Chambord
½   ounce Midori
1   ounce pineapple rum

Grenada is a tiny, but lovely island located far down in the lower Windward Islands. Only 21 miles long by 12 miles wide, there are dozens of secluded beaches and coves, spice plantations, tropical rainforest and charming pastel-colored West Indian structures.

Shake all ingredients well and serve either straight up or over crushed ice.

SKINNY DIPPER

Jamaica

. . . .

1	ounce gold rum
½	ounce Galliano
½	ounce white crème de cacao
1	ounce half and half splash of orange juice

*H*ey mon, welcome to Jamaica! The third largest island in the Caribbean with Cuba and Puerto Rico leading, Jamaica's assets include tropical jungle, breathtaking waterfalls and a wide and diversified terrain. The beaches are of course simply gorgeous, we've all seen them on television and the movies.

Shake all ingredients vigorously and serve straight up or over ice.

STEEL PAN

St. Croix

. . . .

1	ounce passionfruit vodka
1	ounce white rum
4	ounces passionfruit juice granulated sugar

*W*arning, warning! These drinks are so smooth, you'll think you are drinking a fruit drink instead of one heavily laced with alcohol and your head will feel like steel pans are beating in it the next day. Steel pan music is strongly promoted in the islands and actually taught as part of the music program in many schools. My son has been playing in a steel pan band since he was 9 years old and has participated in St. Thomas Carnival parades.

Wet the lip of a rocks glass and twist in the granulated sugar. Fill the glass with ice and pour in all the ingredients, stirring gently.

YELLOW BIRD

Nassau, Bahamas

. . . .

1	ounce light rum
½	ounce pineapple rum
½	ounce crëme de banana
	splash of Galliano
2	ounces pineapple juice
2	ounces orange juice

I absolutely love this tourist song that they named this drink after. Be sure to buy a CD of this and play while serving this and other island drinks to impart just the right atmosphere.

Shake all ingredients and pour into a tall glass filled with ice.

WAVE RUNNER

St. Croix, U. S. Virgin Islands

. . . .

1	ounce lime rum
1	ounce coconut rum
	7-up

St. Croix is the largest of the U. S. Virgin Islands and is the least mountainous of all the islands. Gently rolling hills are dotted with gracious villas and more than 100 sugar mill ruins. During plantation days this island had a tremendous hold on the sugarcane industry in the Caribbean.

Fill a tall glass with ice and stir in the lime and coconut rum. Top off with 7-up.

ZOMBIE

Puerto Rico

. . . .

1	ounce mango rum
1	ounce pineapple rum
1	ounce banana rum
1	ounce light rum
2	ounces orange juice
2	ounces pineapple juice
½	ounce grenadine syrup
	crushed ice

The first time I had a Zombie, I was at the Mad Hatter in Nantucket and only 18 years old. Don't ask me how I managed that since the drinking age was 21 at the time. I guess I looked older than my years back then and now I hope I look at least 10 years younger. This is another one of those drinks that turned up in a cool, dimly lighted bar in Old San Juan, made island-style.

You need to pull out the old blender for this one. Fill with about 1 cup of crushed ice and pour in all the ingredients. Whirl until a slush-like consistency is achieved. Enjoy your visit into the nether world.

BIBLIOGRAPHY

Babb, Dalton. Cooking the West Indian Way. London: The Macmillan Press, Ltd. 1986

Barrow, Errol, W. Privilege Cooking in the Caribbean. U.S.A.: Courage Books. 1998

Berry, Jan. The Art of Preserving. California: Ten Speed Press. 1997

Foley, Ray. Bartending for Dummies. U.S.A.: IDG Books Worldwide, Inc. 1997

Grants, Rosmund. Caribbean and African Cooking. Jamaica: Ian Randle Publishers Ltd. 1988

Grigson, Jane. Exotic Fruits and Vegetables. New York: Henry Holt and Company. 1987

Hamilton, Edward. Rums of the Eastern Caribbean. Puerto Rico: Tafia Publishing 1995

Harris, Dunstan. Island Barbecue Spirited Recipes from the Caribbean. San Francisco: Chronicle Books. 1995

BIBLIOGRAPHY

Henry, Mike. Caribbean Cocktails & Mixed Drinks. Jamaica: Stephansons Litho Press, Ltd. 1980

Marcus, George and Nancy Marcus. Forbidden Fruits and Forgotten Vegetables: A Guide to Cooking with Ethnic, Exotic and Neglected Produce. New York: St. Martin's Press. 1982

Murray, Dea. Cooking with Rum Caribbean Style. U. S. Virgin Islands: Rolfe Associates. 1982

Parkinson, Rosemary. Shake Dat Cocktail. U.S.A.: Courage Books. 1998

Quinn, Lucinda Scala. Jamaica Cooking 140 Roadside and Homestyle Recipes. U.S.A. Macmillan. 1997

Rivera, Oswald. Puerto Rican Cuisine in America. New York: Four Walls Eight Windows. 1993

Rosado, Robert and Judith Rosada. Recipes from La Isla. Chicago: Lowell House, Contemporary Books. 1995

Thomas, Heather. The Essential Caribbean Cookbook. U.S.A.: Courage Books. 1998

INDEX

and servicemark exclusively of McIlhenny Co., Avery Island, LA 70513